How to Care for Your Dwarf Hamster

CONTENTS

Photos by:
**Frank Naylor,
Colin Jeal,
David Alderton**

©2002 by Kingdom Books PO9 5TT ENGLAND
Printed in China through Printworks Int. Ltd.

INTRODUCTION

Dwarf hamsters make lovely pets for young and old alike. They are inexpensive to buy, house and feed, and are easy to care for. However, as with all animals, it is important that any potential owner is fully aware of exactly what is involved in keeping these animals before going ahead with the purchase. You should never buy a pet on a whim, and certainly never give one as a present, unless you know that the recipient wants to become a pet owner. All animals have needs and feelings, and dwarf hamsters are no exception. They may not be as demanding as larger pets such as dogs or cats, but they still need care and attention every day of their lives.

As the name suggests, the dwarf hamster is much smaller than its cousin the Syrian (Golden) hamster and therefore young children may find it difficult to handle. Dwarf hamsters cannot tolerate bad or clumsy handling and a young child, however well-meaning, does not always know his or her own strength. A six-year-old child may be able to handle a dwarf hamster, but ten years and upwards is probably a more suitable age. Also, remember that no child should ever be expected to take sole responsibility for any pet, no matter how many promises are made. All too easily children forget to feed and water their animals, to keep the cage clean and so on, and this is only natural as children are easily distracted. The ultimate responsibility must always rest with an adult (or older teenager), and therefore it follows that you should never buy a dwarf hamster as a pet for a child if you are not prepared to look after it yourself.

Several species of dwarf hamster are available and these vary slightly in size, looks and temperament. Before going to your local pet shop or hamster breeder, you will need to know the differences between the species, and have some idea which type you would prefer to keep as pets.

A Chinese dwarf hamster will be an entertaining pet.

A Normal Winter White Russian dwarf hamster.

The dwarf hamster needs gentle handling.

Campbell's Russian Dwarf Hamster

This dwarf hamster is the one most commonly kept as a pet, and is usually available from any good pet shop. The Campbell's Russian Dwarf is the largest of the dwarf hamsters, measuring approximately 8–10cm (3–4in), sometimes slightly more, and males are usually larger than females. The hamster is plump and round. Its head is short and blunt with tiny ears and large eyes. The legs are very short, and the feet (including their undersides,) are completely covered with fur. The tail is very short and is covered in fur. The fur on the body is dense and soft. In the original variety, as found in the wild, the colour on the body is a pale brown-grey, with a dark slate-grey undercoat. Along the spine runs a darker stripe, starting on the hamster's forehead and extending all the way to the base of the tail. The hamster's belly and underside are nearly white.

Other colour varieties are available, and more are being developed by breeders. These include the **Albino Campbell** which, as the name suggests, is pure white with pink eyes, showing a complete lack of pigment; the **Argente Campbell**, which is a diluted (or 'bleached') version of the normal grey colour – the hamster is orangey/ginger in colour with a grey spinal stripe and pink eyes; the **Mottled Campbell**, which produces a variety of patterns, including spotted, collared, barred, patched and white with very little coloured spotting; and the **Satin Campbell**, which can be any colour and has a characteristic shiny coat which at first glance almost looks wet. Some of the newer colour varieties are the **Platinum** where the fur on the back is heavily ticked in white, giving the hamster a 'silvered' appearance, and the **Dilute Platinum** which looks like a white hamster with black eyes and flesh coloured ears. The **Black** is a new mutation which is being developed in Europe, and in the United States the **Opal** and **Sandy/Black Eyed Argente** are becoming increasingly popular.

Generally, Campbell's Russian Dwarf hamsters are placid and easy to handle. Occasionally, however, you do find a highly-strung animal which can prove difficult to handle and may have a tendency to nip. Therefore it is always a good idea to handle the parents of any dwarf hamster that you intend to buy to get an idea of what their offspring will be like as an adult, as temperament is largely an inherited trait. If this is not possible, which often is the case with hamsters bought from pet shops, try to handle as many different hamsters as possible before making your final choice, carefully selecting the ones that are easiest to handle and show no aggression.

Winter White Russian Dwarf Hamster

This hamster, although similar, is a different sub-species to the Campbell's and is not seen as a pet as frequently as the Campbell's. As the name suggests, the Winter White Russian has the ability to change colour during the cold winter months. All Winter White Russian dwarfs have this ability, regardless of their colour, but it may not happen to your Winter Whites every winter. If the hamsters are kept in cool conditions, such as in a garden shed, they will change colour when the weather gets colder and return to their normal colour as it warms up again. If they are kept in a centrally-heated house, they will remain the same colour all year round.

The Winter White Russian dwarf hamster typically reaches 7–8cm (2.8–3in) and the standard for show animals is 8–10cm (3–4in). The body of the Winter White is less rounded than that of the Campbell's, being bullet-shaped with a raised spine. It is still a round and compact looking animal, with the same short legs, minute tail and furry feet. The eyes are more prominent than that of the Campbell's and the face generally is somewhat longer. In its original form, the colour of the Winter White is more grey than brown, but with the same dark slate undercoat and a jet black dorsal stripe. The belly and underside are white.

An Albino Campbell's Russian.

The original grey colour is the one most commonly seen in Winter White Russians, but new colour varieties are proving popular. The Sapphire is a beautiful blue-grey hamster, with a blue-grey dorsal stripe. The Pearl Winter White is undoubtedly the most beautiful of all dwarf hamsters, as this is a white hamster with black ticking evenly spread all over the hamster's back – not dissimilar to the delicate colouring of the Chinchilla Persian cat. In darker specimens there is a black spinal stripe, but some lighter-coloured Pearls lack this. The eyes are jet black. It is important to know that most male Pearl-coloured Winter Whites are sterile and so cannot be bred from. To produce Pearl offspring, breeders mate a Pearl female to a normal coloured or Sapphire male, which will produce babies of both colours.

The Winter White Russian dwarf usually has an excellent, gentle temperament, making it extremely suitable as a pet.

Chinese Hamsters

Chinese hamsters are not scientifically classified as dwarf hamsters, but are known as 'rat-like' hamsters. They are of dwarf size, and are generally regarded as dwarf hamsters. The Chinese hamster was the first of the dwarf species to be kept as a pet. In appearance, it is very different to the other species of dwarf hamster. The body may be as long as 10cm (4in) and is thin and long, totally lacking the roundness of the Russian hamsters. The face is longer and more mouse-like and the tail, which is virtually hairless, is long in comparison to the body, measuring around 2–3cm (0.75–1in). The legs and feet, although not bald, are covered with very sparse, fine fur and, unlike the Russian varieties, the Chinese hamster has no fur covering the underside of its feet. The fur on the body is slightly shorter than on the Russian varieties, making it more smooth-looking and less fluffy. The ears on a Chinese hamster look larger than on a Russian dwarf because the shorter coat length makes them more prominent, and the eyes are slightly smaller.

The colour of the original Chinese hamster is brown, with a dark slate undercolour. There is a dark spinal stripe, and the belly and underside are near white. The only other variety of the Chinese hamster is the Dominant Spot, which has a varying amount of white spotting on the coloured background. Very rarely, a Dominant Spot animal may show so much white that it looks as though it is entirely white with black eyes.

When Chinese hamsters were first kept, it was feared that they were very aggressive to each other, especially the females to the males. There were many stories of the females attacking, or even killing, the males. However, after a while, two things were discovered. First, some females would eat the bodies of males that died of natural causes and, second, when the hamsters were mated to unrelated hamsters, the aggression seemed to be much reduced.

Chinese hamsters can be tamed down to become pleasant, friendly pets, but this is a more difficult process than with the Russian varieties. As with any animal, if your pet does not want to be tamed, then leave it alone and get your pleasure from simply observing it.

Raborovski's Hamster

This is the final type of dwarf hamster kept as a pet. It is the smallest hamster available, with adults not reaching more than approximately 5cm (2in) in length. Unlike all the other dwarf hamsters, the Raborovski does not have a dark spinal stripe. In its natural form, the colour is a sandy-gold with darker undercolour and a nearly white belly and underside. Its distinctive features are its white 'eyebrows'. It is similar in appearance to the Russian varieties, being a rounded and compact hamster with furry feet and a very short tail. Perhaps the cutest of all hamsters, looking like a miniature hamster or a perpetual baby, the Raborovski is not the most suitable of hamsters as a pet, simply because its small size and very lively temperament make it difficult to handle. These hamsters are usually fairly even tempered, and make suitable pets for the older child or adult who is content to study the hamsters in their cage rather than handle them regularly.

Two Chinese dwarf hamsters. On the left is a Dominant Spot, and a Normal is on the right.

SELECTION

Having decided what type of dwarf hamster you want to keep, the time has come to select your animals. Dwarf hamsters can be found for sale in most pet shops, and breeders often advertise surplus stock in local newspapers.

The first thing to remember when buying your new dwarf hamsters is that if possible they should never be kept singly. Syrian (Golden) hamsters must always be kept on their own as they do not tolerate other hamsters other than at mating times, but this is not true of the dwarf varieties. It is better that they are kept in pairs. If you have a single dwarf already, it will be quite used to living alone so do not put a new hamster in its cage as this will result in serious fighting. When you become more expert at keeping your hamsters, you could try keeping them in small groups.

You should never house two dwarf hamsters of different species together, as this will very seldom work and fighting will occur.

It is very difficult, not to say impossible, to introduce two adult dwarf hamsters to each other, so pairing should always take place when the animals are as young as possible. Dwarf hamsters can be bought from pet shops when they are 5–8 weeks old, and at this age they will readily accept an unrelated companion of similar age. The easiest way to buy a pair of dwarf hamsters that you want to be friends for life is to purchase a couple of litter mates. These are unlikely to fight as they have grown up together.

Dwarf hamsters need company. Buy your hamsters when they are very young, and they will soon get used to each other.

A normal Satin Campbell's Russian. You can clearly see the small ears and large eyes.

Inbreeding is not a problem in animals as small as dwarf hamsters so you can keep a brother and sister together without the risk that they will produce weak offspring. It has to be said that the best combination of dwarf hamsters to keep together is a male and a female. Two males will almost certainly fight once they reach maturity, even though occasionally males are seen to live together happily. Two females will usually share a cage with no problems, but there have been instances where females have fallen out with each other.

Obviously, a male and a female will breed if they are kept together permanently, so bear this in mind when making your selection. (If the hamsters' owner is to be a young child, I would not recommend that he or she starts on hamster breeding.) I have heard of vets managing to neuter male dwarf hamsters, but this is an extremely risky, and expensive, operation for such a small animal as it is likely to die under the anaesthetic. If you have a male and female which have bred and you do not wish to breed any more babies, you must remove the male prior to the birth otherwise the female may very well be pregnant again soon afterwards. A workable solution is to keep a female baby to accompany the mother in one cage, and to keep a father and son in another – fathers and sons often do get on well. However, be very careful as the father will have got used to being by himself, and introducing a new hamster a month later may cause problems.

The dwarf hamster is an engaging, inquisitive animal that will want to know what is going on.

All hamsters fight a little but this rough and tumble is part of their normal play and social behaviour and should not be interfered with. This is different from serious fighting, which you will soon learn to recognise.

Chinese hamsters are by far the most difficult variety to keep as they fall out with each other frequently. If a pair of Chinese start fighting, it is best to separate them and keep them singly, as otherwise they may fight to the death. Never attempt to keep anything but a male and female or two female Chinese together.

When making your actual selection, take care to examine the hamsters as carefully as possible. Hamsters are nocturnal and normally sleep during the day, so do not be put off by a sleepy hamster. The hamster should soon become alert once fully awake. A healthy dwarf hamster has bright, shiny eyes with no signs of any discharge. The fur should be smooth and dense with no bald patches. The nose should be dry, the ears without crustiness, and the area around the tail and anus should be clean. It should not be possible to hear the animal breathe – any rattling noise could indicate breathing problems. As mentioned before, take care to select hamsters that are as easy to handle as possible and do not attempt to nip your fingers. Obviously, young hamsters will not be properly tame and will therefore be pretty lively, but it should still be possible to handle them.

Sexing

Sexing animals as small as dwarf hamsters can be difficult, but any experienced breeder should be able to do this correctly, and the staff in a good pet shop should be able to tell you whether a particular hamster is male or female. The easiest way to sex dwarf hamsters is to compare several, as the differences between the sexes will be more obvious when viewed side by side. Hold the hamster in a firm grip on its back in the palm of your hand. The gap between the anus and genitalia is very short in a female; a male shows at least twice the size gap as a female. In adult males, the testicles can clearly be seen at each side of the tail, especially in Chinese hamsters which have larger testicles than other varieties.

When selecting your hamster - whether male or female - look for bright shiny eyes and smooth dense skin or coat.

EQUIPMENT

A Russian dwarf tries out its travelling cage for size.

You do not need a vast array of equipment for your dwarf hamsters, but certain items are essential. Ideally, you should have purchased these before you bring home your new pets so that the cage is all set up and ready for them to move into immediately upon their arrival.

The Cage

The cage is the most important piece of equipment that your dwarf hamsters will need. Always take great care when choosing a cage, making sure it is totally suitable for its purpose. Pet shops and, in particular, pet superstores, have a large variety of cages from which to choose.

Most cages sold as suitable for hamsters are not suitable for dwarf hamsters. Being such a small animal, a dwarf hamster, especially when a youngster, will be able to squeeze out between the bars of the ordinary hamster cage which has a plastic bottom tray and wire canopy. Even if the hamster looks as though it is too big to get out, it may be able to as hamsters are regular little escape artists. If possible, always avoid cages with wire canopies for this reason.

Cages are available especially for mice and dwarf hamsters that have very little space between each bar, and these make suitable homes. The space between each bar must be no more than 0.5cm. A cage like this will make a perfect home for a pair of dwarf hamsters provided that it is at least 40 x 30cm (16 x 12in) in size. The general rule is, the bigger the cage, the better. For a pair of breeding dwarf hamsters I would not recommend anything smaller than 50 x 50cm (20 x 20in) as they will need space to rear their family. Fights between dwarf hamsters are also far more likely to occur in a small, cramped cage. From the owner's point of view, a large cage will need cleaning out less frequently, so will save time.

The best type of housing for dwarf hamsters is without a doubt the cage which has a deep plastic base (either coloured or see-through) with a plastic, see-through top and a fine wire lid. The lid has bars too narrow for any dwarf hamster to escape through and, as the cage has no bars on the sides, no shavings or other bedding will fall out, making it a favourite for the house-proud hamster owner. This sort of cage is easy to keep clean, and it will give your hamsters some privacy.

Alternatively, an empty fish tank of a suitable size made either from glass or plastic will make a good cage, provided that you make a lid from very fine mesh to fit securely over the top. Even if the tank is a tall one, an ingenious dwarf hamster will find a way to climb out if there is no lid. A glass tank will be quite heavy to handle when it needs to be cleaned out, so a plastic one is preferable.

A ceramic boot makes a good toy for these two Russians.

Avoid home-made wooden cages as hamsters are rodents and will chew wood.

The bottom of the cage should be filled with clean, white wood shavings, which are available from pet shops. Do not use sawdust as the fine particles will find their way into the hamsters' eyes and noses. Newspaper or cat litter should not be used either, as they may cause problems such as allergies and sore feet. Bedding can take the form of either soft tissue paper or simply the wood shavings, as the hamsters can easily manufacture a bed out of this. Always avoid cotton wool-type bedding or bedding made of natural fibres or hay. Such material can wrap itself around the hamster's legs, cutting off the blood supply, or can choke the hamster if it attempts to put it inside its cheek pouches; sharp points of hay may injure the hamster's eyes.

Other Equipment

Your dwarf hamsters will need a ceramic bowl for food. Ceramic is the only material that the hamsters will not be able to chew or topple over. A gravity water bottle is essential because the hamsters should always have a ready supply of clean water to drink. Do not use a bowl for water, as this will soon be contaminated with shavings and food.

A Russian dwarf albino with her young.

This Argente Campbell's Russian dwarf hamster is enjoying investigating the flower pots.

A small house of some sort is appreciated by all dwarf hamsters, and is essential when they have babies. The house can take many shapes. An old cardboard box will do the trick, but this will have to be replaced regularly as it will be chewed. Half an empty coconut with a small opening cut at the front makes an excellent house. A variety of houses are available from pet shops.

An exercise wheel is greatly appreciated by these busy little rodents. This does not need to be very big; 10–13cm (4–5in) in diameter is ideal. The best sort is a plastic wheel with a solid back.

For transporting your hamsters, or for somewhere to put them when you clean out the cage, a small carrying box is ideal. This is a clear plastic box with a coloured lid with air vents in. They come in many different sizes and you can buy one cheaply from a pet shop.

As for toys, your hamsters will appreciate empty cardboard rolls, empty light bulb boxes, eggboxes and similar items, and small, clean branches from fruit trees that they can chew.

FEEDING

Your dwarf hamsters should always have food and water available in their cage, as they like to nibble at their food on and off throughout the day. Like all hamsters, they have a cheek pouch on each side of their head which they use to transport food. Dwarf hamsters do not use these pouches as frequently as Syrian hamsters, but you will notice that they will collect their favourite food inside their cheek pouches, carry it into their house or nest, and store it in there to eat later. It is important to realise that food and water must be available at all times, because dwarf hamsters are such small animals that they very quickly dehydrate and lose weight if left without water and food even for just a few hours.

The main diet for your dwarf hamsters should consist of a good quality hamster mix. You can buy this from any pet shop and many pet food market stalls, and even larger supermarkets sell hamster mixes. A good mix contains wheat, pellets, flaked maize, flaked peas, peanuts, sunflower seeds and similar items. Hamsters do require a fair amount of protein in their diet, so should never be fed on mixes intended for rabbits or guinea pigs as these simply do not contain enough protein.

Serve the hamster mix in a bowl in the hamster's cage, and top it up daily. Do not make the mistake of thinking that your hamsters still have plenty of food left simply because certain ingredients from the mix remain in the bowl – many hamsters have strong preferences for which food they like and may refuse to eat part of their hamster mix. Top up the food bowl daily, and throw away any remaining food every time the cage is cleaned out.

Other than hamster mix, your dwarf hamsters will need supplements at least several times a week, but preferably daily. These can take the form of fruit or vegetable pieces such as carrot, apple, cabbage, cucumber, grapes, banana, tomato and so on. Left-over food from your own dinner can make excellent supplementary hamster food (as long as it is not too spicy) as hamsters are omnivorous and will eat virtually anything. Suitable food includes boiled potatoes, pasta, bread, rice, eggs, pancakes, fish fingers, sausages, meatballs, ham, turkey and chicken. Even the occasional piece of pizza can be given, as long as it has no garlic in it. (This is not to prevent your hamster's breath from smelling, but because garlic thins the blood which may cause a problem in an animal as small as the dwarf hamster.)

Hamster mix provides a good basic food.

Food that must never be given includes anything spicy, citrus fruits, onions, sweets or chocolate. All of these will endanger your hamster's health. Never be tempted to give your hamster doggy chocolate drops, either. Chocolate will melt in the cheek pouches which will cause the hamster great problems as it will not be able to remove the sticky mess.

Dog biscuits, such as the type filled with marrow, make good hamster treats and are very suitable for the hamsters to exercise their teeth on. However, dry dog biscuits of the type that are meant to be soaked in water before feeding must be avoided. If fed dry, the biscuits may expand inside the hamster's stomach and could even kill it.

Water is the best drink for adult hamsters, but milk is a suitable supplement for young dwarf hamsters, pregnant females or mothers with suckling babies. This can be cow's milk, goat's milk, or milk substitutes for pets. Do not give non-breeding adult hamsters milk of any sort, as it can cause stomach upsets. Never give your hamsters fizzy drinks or alcohol 'for a joke' as, if they are tempted to drink it, it will make them ill.

Clean water must always be available from a water bottle clipped to the outside of the cage.

BREEDING

The breeding of any animal should never be undertaken lightly. Always consider your decision carefully. Will you find good homes for the baby hamsters that you are hoping to breed? Dwarf hamsters normally breed every 21 days and, although the litters generally are small (4–6 babies), numbers will soon grow. The largest number in a litter I have ever known was eight, but this is rare. It is not unusual for dwarfs to have 6–10 litters during the female's fertile year. Many pet shops will be happy to buy the baby hamsters off you, but I strongly advise that you check this out in advance, so that you do not suddenly find yourself with dozens of hamsters that nobody wants.

Breeding dwarf hamsters is comparatively easy. As dwarf hamsters pair for life, simply place the male and the female together as youngsters, and leave them to get on with the breeding. The male will stay with the female at all times. Thus it follows that a pair of dwarf hamsters may produce as often as once a month, but this is far from the norm. Most dwarf hamsters will produce a litter now and then, perhaps four or so during an entire year. Somehow, the hamsters know when to take a break, and the female will not get pregnant despite being mated. With others, you may find that they will never breed, or will only breed one litter in an entire lifetime.

A female dwarf hamster.

The female dwarf hamster may give birth to her first litter at around the age of four months, or she may wait until she is six to eight months of age. The average pregnancy lasts for about 21 days.

Females do not show many physical signs of pregnancy and perhaps the first indication you get of the birth is when you hear tiny little squeaks, and find a litter of newborn baby hamsters inside the parents' nest. Sometimes the mother may chase the male away for a couple of days and, if you see him in an unusual place, this might indicate she has given birth. Most dwarf hamster litters consist of an average of four babies, occasionally as many as six. The parents will take turns in looking after the babies, washing them and keeping them warm. The cage must be kept in a quiet spot so that the parents are not disturbed; it is not unknown for frightened or stressed hamsters to kill their offspring in a misguided attempt to protect them from some perceived danger. Avoid vacuuming or making other sudden noises near the cage for at least the first 10 days. Never touch newborn baby hamsters as this may also cause insecure parents to kill and eat them. Leave the cleaning of the cage until the babies are old enough to have left the nest.

Baby hamsters are born deaf, blind and naked. The fur will start to grow after a couple of days and, by the age of one week, they will be completely covered in fur.

A male dwarf hamster.

At about the same age, the babies will start to show an interest in solid food and you can sprinkle oatflakes over the nest for them to eat. The parents will also bring them food. Make sure to serve plenty of food, preferably of a kind that is suitable for the tiny babies such as lettuce, pasta, bread and so on.

At 14 days, the babies will open their eyes, and will start to wander out of their nest. At first, the parents will attempt to put them back inside the nest, but they will soon realise that this exercise is pointless! The babies will suckle from their mother for at least another week. At four weeks old they will be fully weaned and fully formed, looking like miniatures of their parents. This is the time to separate them from their parents, as the parents will have grown tired of them and may also have a new litter on the go. Sometimes a new litter is born after only three weeks, and in such a case the older litter should be removed.

Although weaning is not a particularly stressful time for young dwarf hamsters, if they are sent to another home too early the new routine and food might cause them to suffer from diarrhoea. It is better to keep them for another week so that

One day old baby Russians.

they continue with the same routine, rather than being moved too early to another household which will add further stress. The babies can safely go to their new homes when they are 4–5 weeks old.

Most dwarf hamster females will stop breeding at around the age of 12 months, although males are fertile for a few months longer.

Now the babies are 16 days old. A Normal is on the left, and a Platinum is on the right.

GENERAL CARE

Try to get into a routine of caring for your hamsters. They will soon get to know when you are around.

Siting The Cage

Make sure the cage is placed in a suitable place. A child will probably want to keep the cage in his or her bedroom, and this is fine as long as the actual spot is one where the hamsters will not be constantly disturbed. A quiet corner of the room, perhaps on top of a small table or chest of drawers, is ideal. Remember that hamsters are nocturnal and prefer to sleep for most of the day, becoming active in the evening. The cage should not be placed on the floor, as it may be kicked by mistake and often the floor is draughty. Nor should it be placed close to a window, as the sun may cause it to overheat, and the draught from the window could cause the hamsters to catch cold or get runny eyes in the winter.

A favourite spot for the hamster cage is on top of the work surface in the kitchen, although naturally not too close to the cooker. This is a room which usually is most active in the evening, and the hamsters will soon get used to seeing people around. They will also appreciate being fed table scraps!

An Argente Campbell's on a deep bed of wood shavings.

If you intend to breed hamsters, and therefore need to keep large numbers, a garden shed is usually the best place for all your cages. These can be placed on suitable shelving. Care must be taken that the shed does not get too hot in the summer or too cold in the winter, and it should be as draught-proof as possible. A single cage of pet dwarf hamsters is far better kept indoors where people can see the animals.

Remember that other pets, such as dogs or cats, must not be able to reach the hamsters' cage. Most dogs will leave dwarf hamsters alone, especially if the cage is placed above floor level, but all cats will regard dwarf hamsters as easy prey, and will do everything they can to get to the animals. If you own cats, the cage ought to be kept inside a room to which they have no access.

A family group of mother and babies.

Taming Your Dwarf Hamsters

Naturally, you will want your dwarf hamsters to be tame, friendly and easy to handle. With patience, most dwarf hamsters soon become tame pets that will enjoy being handled by their owner.

When you arrive home with your dwarf hamsters from the pet shop or breeder, put them straight into their cage and then leave them alone for 24 hours. Do not attempt to handle them at all, as they will need time to get used to their new home and adjust to the unfamiliar surroundings, unusual noises, feeding routine and so on.

Once your hamsters have settled down in their new home, the taming process can start. Don't attempt to rush things, as this will only stress your hamsters and make them wary of you. Do not make any sudden movements, or loud noises. Stand next to the cage (or sit with it on the floor) and put your hand inside it. Have some tasty treat, such as a couple of peanuts or sunflower seeds, in the palm of your hand, and keep still. The dwarf hamsters will soon smell the food and will be curious enough to walk up to your hand to investigate. It should not be long before they take the food readily from your hand. Once they have got used to your hand, you can start handling them. Wait for a hamster to climb onto the palm of your hand, and then gently close your fingers around its body and lift it out of the cage. The hamster will want to walk away so you will need to let it walk as if on a treadmill with you continuously moving one hand in front of the other. Soon the hamster will get used to being in your hands, and will not attempt to walk away. Alternatively, grab the hamster gently by placing your hand over it and take a firm – but not too tight – grip of the body. The hamster is so small that you will be able to cover its entire body with your hand.

Most dwarf hamsters will soon get used to being handled. In the rare instances that they do not, you may have to settle for just watching them inside their cage, perhaps letting them take food off your hand. If you find it absolutely impossible to handle the hamsters, you can use a small fishing net to catch them when you need to clean out the cage, although obviously this should be a last resort.

Never attempt to wake a sleeping dwarf hamster, as it will be startled and will probably try to bite you. A frightened hamster will lie on its back, screech and show its teeth. If this happens, leave well alone until it has settled down.

Dwarf hamsters are far too small to be able to take exercise outside their cage. If you let them loose on the floor they may find a hole or crack in a wall somewhere and will never be seen again. With a large cage and an exercise wheel, your dwarf hamsters will get all the exercise they need.

Cleaning The Cage

How often you need to clean out your hamsters' cage will depend on the size. Naturally, a small cage will become soiled much quicker than a large one. A medium-sized cage of approximately 40 x 30cm (16 x 12in) usually will need cleaning once a week. Probably you will find that your dwarf hamsters use a particular corner of their cage as a toilet area, and this corner you can clean out daily, removing the soiled wood shavings and replacing with fresh. When cleaning out the entire cage, the hamsters will need to be removed to a safe place, such as a carrying box (see Equipment).

Remove all the shavings and bedding and replace with new, fresh material. You will find that a paint scraper is a very useful tool to scrape away soiled shavings. Remove all uneaten fresh food, such as vegetables, from the hamsters' nest but, if possible, leave some dry favourites such as peanuts or biscuits, as the hamsters will be upset if they return to a clean cage to find that their entire store of food has gone. Clean out bowls and the water bottle and, if necessary, wash the cage bottom with water and a suitable, non-toxic detergent.

Other Care

Other than feeding, handling and cleaning the cage, your dwarf hamsters will not normally need any other care. Their coats are short and need no grooming from you, as the hamsters will do all this themselves, carefully licking and grooming themselves several times a day. If you do feel that you need to do some extra

An Argente Campbell's Russian dwarf introduces her babies to hamster mix.

grooming, an old toothbrush is excellent for this purpose. Claws will only need trimming on rare occasions (see Health). Hamsters should never be bathed, as the chill will probably give them pneumonia. Dwarf hamsters are very clean little animals, and what little smell they have is natural. If the cage smells, it is simply because you do not clean it often enough!

A pregnant dwarf hamster looking just a little rounder than usual.

HEALTH

Properly cared for, dwarf hamsters are healthy little animals which seldom fall ill. This chapter is a general guide to health problems only; if you are ever unsure about your hamster's health, you should always see a vet.

A healthy dwarf hamster lives for between 18 months and two years, sometimes a little longer. The Raborovski normally lives 2–3 years, sometimes longer.

Colds

If exposed to draughts, dwarf hamsters can catch colds which may turn into pneumonia. This is very serious and will lead to the death of the hamster if not treated promptly. Always keep your hamsters' cage in a draught-proof place, not too close to any window or door. A hamster with a cold will be lethargic, perhaps huddling in a corner of its cage. It will have a rough, unkempt-looking coat, and its back will be hunched up. The nose and eyes will show a discharge and the hamster will breathe noisily. Place the cage in a warm spot, such as close to a radiator, and give the hamster some lukewarm milk mixed with water and bit of honey. If the hamster will not drink, you must feed it with a syringe or eye dropper. If there is no improvement within 24 hours, you must see a vet.

Most healthy dwarf hamsters live for up to two years, sometimes longer.

A female spotted Chinese hamster.

Sore Eyes

This common complaint is usually caused by some injury to the eyes or an infection caused by a draught. The eye (or eyes) will show a discharge and may appear red and sore. Bathe the eye with a boric acid solution three times a day, using an eye dropper. Mix half a cupful of boiling water with a teaspoon of boric acid powder (available from chemists), stir until the water is clear, and allow to cool to blood heat. If no improvement is seen within a couple of days, see a vet. Occasionally, a very badly damaged eye will shrivel up and fall out. This doesn't normally cause the hamster any great problems, and veterinary attention is seldom needed.

Broken Limbs

Occasionally, a dwarf hamster may break a leg by falling from a great height. It is not usually possible (or necessary) to plaster or splint such a tiny leg, and the hamster will not appear to be in great discomfort. Simply keep the hamster in a small cage minus the exercise wheel and no objects to climb on until the leg has healed which will take about two weeks.

Heatstroke

Heatstroke is caused by over-exposure to sun and/or heat. The hamster will collapse, and its fur will look wet. The immediate action is to spray a fine mist of cool water all over the hamster, particularly over its head. Take care not to drown it, though! Hopefully, the hamster will come round and recover completely, but sometimes it will die if not treated in time as heatstroke will cause the hamster to dehydrate and this in turn can lead to kidney failure. Always prevent this condition by keeping the cage away from heat and direct sunlight.

Diarrhoea

A dwarf hamster's droppings are normally black and very firm to the touch. The sign of diarrhoea is when the droppings are loose and watery. Diarrhoea is normally caused by overfeeding with wet vegetables, such as lettuce, cucumber or tomatoes, but it can also be caused by stress. It is best treated by leaving the hamster without wet food until its stomach settles, just feeding a dry mix and water. Arrowroot biscuits may also help.

Wounds

Wounds are usually caused by fights between two hamsters. Bathe any wound twice a day with a suitable antiseptic solution such as Savlon or iodine, and make sure that the hamster is kept in a clean cage. If the wounds are very deep or take a long time to heal, see a vet.

Overgrown Claws

This sometimes occurs as the hamster reaches an advanced age. Carefully trim the claws with a pair of nail clippers suitable for babies. You will be able to see the quick as a dark pink line inside the claw; cut just beyond this. If you are unsure, ask your vet for advice.

Tumours

These sometimes occur in hamsters and show as a swelling or lump anywhere in the body. It is virtually impossible to remove a tumour successfully from such a small animal, so it is best to leave it alone. If the tumour appears to cause the hamster pain, or grows so large that the hamster finds it difficult to move, it is kinder to let your vet put the hamster to sleep.

This young Russian dwarf is enjoying its exercise.

Dwarf hamsters are far too small to be able to take exercise outside their cage. With a large cage and an exercise wheel, your dwarf hamsters will get all the exercise they need.

Parasites

Hamsters sometimes suffer from parasites, both external (such as mites) and internal (worms). A hamster with external parasites will suffer from fur loss, scaly skin, and may itch. As hamsters should not be bathed, the best way for this to be treated is by giving the drug Ivermectin, which either can be given orally (mixed with the water in the hamster's water bottle), or as an injection given by your vet. It is perfectly safe for hamsters. Worms will cause the hamster to suffer from loose droppings, an extended belly, poor fur and poor general condition; actual worms may sometimes be seen. Roundworms are the usual culprits and they can be eradicated by buying any over-the-counter liquid wormer which is suitable for kittens, and mixing the recommended dose for kittens with a full bottle of the hamster's drinking water.

A dwarf hamster perched on a 35mm film canister shows the small size of these animals.

FURTHER READING

Further Reading:

Guide to Owning A Hamster
by Anmarie Barrie
ISBN - 0793821541
Softcover: 250mm x 170mm, 64 Pages
Full colour throughout.

Really Useful Hamster Guide
by Lorraine Hill
ISBN - 1852791306
Hardcover: 260mm x 180mm, 48 pages
Full colour illustrations throughout.

Quick & Easy Guide to Hamsters
ISBN - 0793810264
Softcover: 215mm x 140mm, 64 pages
Full colour throughout.

Collins Family Pet Guide Series - Hamster
by David Alderton
ISBN - 0007122829
Softcover: 210mm x 150mm, 128 pages
Full colour throughout.

All of these titles are available from:
Pet Marketing Services,
PO Box 74,
Havant
PO9 5TT UK
Customer order line - ++44 (0)2392 481166